The reproductive system of female birds consists of the ovaries and oviduct. The yolk is produced by the ovaries, while egg white and shell are added in the oviduct. The testicles of male birds are inside the abdominal cavity and cannot be seen or felt from outside, unlike in mammals. Male cockatiels do not have a penis. Mating is achieved by the male and female pressing or rubbing together their cloacas.

A normal grey cock.

BUYING

Judging the health of any animal requires experience and a bit of good luck. Ask friends, other bird keepers and your local veterinary surgeon about reliable pet shops and breeders although, of course, you will have to use your own judgement following the general impression you get from the seller. Does the seller seem confident with the birds? Are the premises clean, tidy and draught-free? It is best to let the seller handle the animals as in this way accidents are prevented and you can gain an idea of how familiar he or she is with the birds.

Healthy Birds

Before getting close to the aviary or cage, stand back and watch what is going on. Healthy birds are alert, hop from perch to perch, and show natural shyness when a stranger approaches. Lack of shyness is often a sign of illness, not of tameness. Respiration should be quiet and even. An open beak, heavy or distressed breathing, and a watery or creamy discharge from the eyes and nostrils are signs of a respiratory disease.

The plumage should be smooth and shiny, and the feathers should not show any defects. The feathers around the vent should be dry and clean. Dirty vent feathers are usually a sign of intestinal or kidney problems. The droppings of a normal, healthy cockatiel are green and firm with a white 'cap', which is the material excreted by the kidneys.

Feel the bird's breast muscles; a bird with a sharply-protruding breast bone is underweight and probably ill. Reject any bird with fluffed-up plumage, ocular or nasal discharge, defective feathers, crusty skin, dirty vent, overgrown beak, missing toes or laboured breathing.

How Many Birds?

In my opinion, a pair or group of birds is preferable because it means more enjoyment for the birds, and thus for the bird keeper - for there is no doubt that it is entertaining to watch how these cheerful birds behave with each other. Wild cockatiels live in small flocks, so mixing sexes is normally no problem, except during the breeding season. A slight disadvantage to this is that the birds will spend more time with each other than with the owner and are likely to become less tame than would a single bird.

You must remember that a cockatiel with no other companions needs a lot of attention from its owner. A bird left alone for long periods of time tends to become frustrated and depressed, and it might start plucking its own feathers, which is an almost impossible habit to break once it starts.

How to Care for Your Cockatiel

CONTENTS

We would like to thank the following for permission to photograph their stock:
Hansards Pet Centre, Romsey
Mick Coates
Mrs Cowell, Portsmouth

Photographs by:
Frank Naylor
Colin Jeal

KINGDOM

©2001 by Kingdom Books PO9 5TT ENGLAND

GENERAL

Some knowledge of how cockatiels live in their natural habitat of Australia should help us to understand cockatiels kept in captivity under different geographical and climatic conditions. However, most cockatiels today come from breeding stocks of birds which have been used to a captive, domestic environment for many years. Therefore we do not have to provide a reproduction in miniature of Australian conditions for our pet to feel well and to breed. We do, however, have to keep the cockatiel's native environment in mind.

Wild cockatiels are largely nomadic; they live in small groups in the more subtropical parts of Australia and in the dry grass and bush typical of the inner part of the continent. Their diet consists of half-ripe and ripe grasses and herb seeds, which they can find on the ground, and also of green foods that grow during the lush rainy season, when cockatiels normally breed. However, cockatiels will breed whenever conditions are favourable, sometimes several times in succession. Nests are built in tree holes, always close to water holes or small streams.

Temperatures in continental Australia vary from well above 40°C (104°F) to below freezing at night so cockatiels are quite a hardy species used to varying conditions. Nevertheless, they cannot survive under the climatic conditions of Northern Europe and North America without our help.

Structure And Function Of Birds

Structure (anatomy) and function (physiology) of birds and mammals are similar, but there are some important differences.

Avian skin is very thin; it has no sweat glands or sebaceous glands and is covered by feathers. Occasionally the feathers are changed during the process known as moulting. During moulting, old feathers are shed and new ones grow in their place. In cockatiels, moulting is a very gradual process, extending over several months, and may not be noticed by the owner.

The respiratory system of birds consists basically of the trachea, bronchi and lungs, as it does in mammal species. Additionally, birds have thin air sacs (sac-like protrusions from the lungs into the chest and abdominal cavity) which can play an important role during the course of respiratory diseases.

The avian digestive system consists of an oral cavity, oesophagus and crop, proventriculus, gizzard and relatively short intestines. Birds do not have teeth, but cockatiels do husk large seeds before swallowing them. The food is ground in the strong, muscular gizzard that all herbivorous birds possess. This grinding action is helped by sand and small stones, called grit, which the birds swallow either with their food or intentionally if they can find them. Sometimes a bird mistakes lead shot, sharp pieces of metal, plastic or glass for grit, which usually leads to chronic poisoning or painful internal injuries from which the bird may die.

Sexing the cockatiel: the normal grey hen on the left has a predominantly grey head with dull orange ear patches while the cock on the right has a bright yellow head with bright orange ear patches. The hen also has yellow bars on the underside of her tail which the cock does not.

Sexing The Cockatiel

If you want only one cockatiel, you do not have to worry about its sex as both sexes make good pets. If you want a breeding pair, it is important to know how to sex cockatiels. Sexing young cockatiels can take a lot of practice, so get help from someone with experience if you are unsure. Adult males of the 'normal' wild-type are relatively easy to distinguish from adult females: the males have yellow heads and crests with bright orange ear patches, while the hens have grey heads and dull orange ear patches. In adult females the underside of the tail is barred with yellow.

However, these differences in cockatiels are not visible until after the first moult, which is between three and nine months of age. Until then, young males resemble the adult females. This is unfortunate because the best time to acquire a cockatiel is when it is still young. Mating behaviour is a further indication of a bird's sex: male birds will try to mate (tread) the female partner.

Sexing can be a bit more difficult in some of the colour forms that have been developed in recent years. With the Lutino, for example, you may have to hold the bird in your hand to identify such characteristics as the darker yellow bars on the hen's tail feathers. The lively song of the cock can also help you identify the sex.

Age

It is better to acquire a cockatiel while it is still young, adaptable and able to learn, although older birds can make very good pets as well. Determining the age of a bird is a difficult task, even for experts. Unlike many mammals, birds do not have teeth or skin wrinkles that can indicate the age of the individual. Young chicks have somewhat duller colours and shorter tail feathers than adult birds. Newly-fledged birds have a bald patch behind the crest, giving

Left: In the nest box, parent with three-day-old chick and unhatched eggs.

a good indication of age up to about three months. The skin around the nostrils (*cere*) is pink during the first months, and then turns progressively grey-black, except in Lutinos and Red-eyed Silver cockatiels, where it remains pink.

Very old birds lose the shiny appearance of their leg scales and plumage, and find it increasingly difficult to keep their balance on the perch. Some joints, particularly foot joints, may swell due to gout.

Colour Mutations

Several interesting mutations of the wild-type cockatiel have appeared in recent decades. The first mutation was the *Pied Cockatiel*, in which the colour varies from predominantly grey to almost white. The *Lutino* was first bred in Florida. The colour is pale lemon; the grey is completely lost, but the bird still has the orange ear patches.

Pearls are a Lutino mutation. They have a varying amount of grey feathers within the lemon-coloured plumage. Cocks lose most of this pearled appearance after their first moult and then resemble the normal wild-type cockatiel. Some other mutations are the pale-brown *Cinnamon*, *Red-eyed Silver*, *White-faced*, and *Blue* cockatiels. These mutations are attractive birds but offer no advantages other than colour over the standard wild-type cockatiel.

Your New Bird At Home

Carry your new cockatiel in a container or cage which is draught-free and strong enough to hold together if the bird attacks it with its beak.

Keep the newcomer separate from other birds and under observation (*in quarantine*) until you are convinced that it is healthy. Nevertheless, even a quarantined bird may carry disease without showing symptoms and you must monitor it after it has joined the other birds.

Apart from the danger of infectious diseases, the new bird may also have problems adjusting to its new environment and may be harassed by other birds or itself prove to be a bully. Put the newcomer in a small cage within the aviary for a few days so that you can watch its behaviour, and thus prevent some of these problems.

Other Birds And Pets

Cockatiels are normally quite peaceful birds, but there may be arguments about partners and good nesting spots. Cockatiels mix well with many other small avian species such as canaries, budgerigars, finches and other small parrots, but they should be separated from larger psittacine birds, which may attack them.

Cockatiels can be kept with dogs as long as the dogs are trained to leave them alone, but should be permanently caged away from cats. If you let your cockatiel out among any other pets, make sure they cannot hurt your bird. Also make sure that fish tanks are covered and none of the plants in the room are poisonous.

A six-week-old cockatiel being handled.
Birds intended as pets should be purchased as young as possible.

Pied mutation cockatiels.

HOUSING

The cockatiel needs a large, roomy cage, at least 60 x 50 x 40cm (24 x 20 x 16in) in size, so that it can spread its wings without touching the cage wire. If the cage is too small, the bird may not get enough exercise and will become fat or otherwise unhealthy. Many, if not most, of the standard cages for budgerigars are too small (even for budgerigars) but larger parrot cages often prove suitable. The cage wire should be arranged horizontally on at least two sides for the bird to climb up, and the spacing of the wire should be narrow enough to prevent young birds from getting their heads stuck between the bars. Some parrot keepers and veterinary surgeons dislike round cages, which they say disorient the bird and lead to circling disease. Proper furnishing might prevent this, but would further reduce the space, which is already considerably smaller in round cages than in rectangular ones.

Metal is most commonly used for the upper wire unit of the cage, while plastic is used for the bottom unit. The bottom unit is either attached to the upper wire by catches or consists of a sliding tray, which makes cleaning easier. Some cages are made of brass but this copper alloy may develop a toxic green deposit (*verdigris*) on its surface. Apart from this, some people feel that the golden appearance of brass detracts from the bird.

Timber and bamboo cages, commonly seen in Asian countries, must be avoided because organic material is very difficult to keep clean, offers hiding places for parasites and cannot stand up to the strength of a cockatiel's beak. Freshly galvanized cage and aviary wire should be avoided if possible. Droplets of zinc, a toxic metal, may form and be broken off and swallowed by the birds. Birds under stress are particularly prone to do this to relieve their anxiety. Screening or lining the sides of the cage prevents messy scattering of seeds and husks. The liner material should not be made of glass and it should be strong enough to withstand the bird's beak.

Sand And Grit

Under natural conditions cockatiels feed mostly on the ground, where they find the grass seeds that make up most of their diet. Therefore, cockatiels should have access to the bottom of their cage. Metal grills, sometimes recommended for hygienic reasons, prevent this and should not be used. The risk of catching an infectious disease from the droppings at the bottom of the cage is minimal as long as the recommended cleaning procedure is followed. Also, most brands of bird sand contain pieces of grated mussel and eggshells for the bird's mineral metabolism and sand and small stones to help the gizzard with its grinding.

Gravel paper, ie paper with sand or seeds glued onto it, may help to keep the bird's toenails short but does not satisfy the cockatiel's natural desire to pick and scratch on the floor. Neither does it soften the impact of the bird's landing on the floor, which might be considerable because the bird cannot make full use of its wings inside the cage. Therefore, bird sand is better than gravel paper for the cockatiel.

A young hand-tamed lutino cockatiel just taking off from its owner's hand.

Perches

Perches in commercially available cages are made usually of dowelled timber or moulded plastic and have a standard diameter. It is good practice to replace these standard diameter perches with natural branches. For cockatiels, the perch diameter should vary between 0.5 and 2.0cm, forcing the bird to adjust its toe muscles constantly. The branch can be from a variety of deciduous trees such as fruit, elm, willow, beech and larch trees, to name but a few. Never use branches from shrubs or trees with bitter or toxic branches, fruit or bark. Make sure the branch is free of droppings from wild birds and wash it before putting it inside the cage. Never put branches treated with pesticides inside the cage. Apart from forcing the bird to exercise its toe muscles, natural branches also keep the bird amused and serve as an important supplement to the diet, because cockatiels gnaw and eat the bark or rind, which contains nutrients. Once the natural branch is chewed clean, replace it with a new one.

Arrange the perches to allow maximum freedom of movement within the already restricted space of the cage. Two branches at least 40cm (16in) apart with no obstacle between them, forces the bird to use its wings to get from one perch to the other. Also, there should be at least 10cm (4in) of empty space between the perch and the end of the cage, otherwise the tail feathers will rub against the wire as the bird turns. Do not fit perches above feed or water containers because the bird's waste may drop into its food and water, contaminating them.

Necessary Accessories

Necessary cage accessories include water bottles, food containers, bathing facilities and cuttlefish bones. Toys can be useful if they offer your bird entertainment and encourage it to exercise; but some toys are less useful or even superfluous, doing little more than using up space inside the cage.

The most common type of drinker is the plastic bottle with metal spout. This type of drinker clips to the side of the cage and relies on gravity to bring water to the tip of the spout, which often has a metal ball as a stopper. The spout must be made of a durable material such as metal, as sharp pieces of broken plastic can be ingested and lead to internal injuries and possibly death. Clean the drinker regularly, as algae tends to grow inside it. Other types of water containers are open cups made of heavy plastic or earthenware materials. Do not place drinking water on the floor as it can easily become contaminated by the bird's droppings. Change the drinking water itself at least twice daily, otherwise certain bacteria (coli, staphylococcal, and others) get a chance to multiply rapidly, particularly under warm conditions. Water contaminated in this way may lead to severe and often lethal crop and gut infections, or the bird refuses to drink altogether and dehydrates.

Baths are either transparent bath houses or shallow tip-proof saucers placed on the floor. The water must be tepid and must be changed daily. Remove saucers after bath time to prevent the cage getting wetter. Do not use antiparasitic bath additives, unless ectoparasites are diagnosed, as birds usually drink from the water in which they are going to bathe. Tame birds enjoy a spray with lukewarm water several times a week. Do not spray your bird just before its sleeping time and wet only the outer feathers (coverts), not the soft down feathers underneath, otherwise it might catch a chill.

Feeders should be made of earthenware or heavy plastic to prevent the bird breaking them up and ingesting the pieces. Usually they are fitted on the inside of the cage, but some breeders like to offer the feed in heavy, tip-proof earthenware saucers on the floor because, in their natural habitat, cockatiels feed mainly on the ground. The disadvantage is that the feed becomes soiled with droppings.

Single or small numbers of birds are fed the usual seed mixture but this is probably too wasteful for larger groups, as individual birds tend to be choosy, sticking to one or a few types of seeds, rejecting and spilling the others. Many keepers with large numbers of cockatiels find it cheaper to store the various seeds that make up the birds' diet separately so there is less waste. From time to time, blow the empty husks from the top of the seed containers to make sure that there is sufficient feed left. Fresh or green feed, fruit and vegetables should be offered in a separate container or clipped to the cage wire, but must be removed before they spoil.

Cuttlefish bone belongs in every cage. It is usually clipped to the cage wire. The bird uses it to trim its beak and as a source of calcium and phosphorus.

Cockatiels like toys, but do not give them so many that the cage is over-crowded.

Various toys are available for the amusement of birds (and bird keepers) at your pet shop, including entire playgrounds, swings, bells, mirrors and ladders. As long as they do not restrict the bird's movements and are made of unbreakable material they serve a useful purpose, but do not overload the interior of the cage.

Nest boxes have to be provided for a breeding pair and should be approximately 25 x 25cm (10 x 10in) at the base and 30cm (12in) high. They should have a shallow depression for the eggs at the bottom, an entrance hole of 8 to 10cm (2.4 to 4in) in diameter, a perch outside the entrance hole, and an inspection flap on the top. A rough surface or wire mesh on the outside of the nest box helps the young cockatiels as they learn to climb.

Nest box hygiene is critically important to the survival of the nestlings and to their future development and health. Nest boxes should be easy to clean and must be cleaned and disinfected before each new clutch. Brooding temperature and humidity inside the nest box favour the growth of fungi, which can cause lethal respiratory infections. Large crevices and cracks may cause draughts which chill the nestlings, and offer ectoparasites good hiding places. Make sure that the inspection flap is closed properly at all times because chilling from above is a common cause of deaths among nestlings. The nesting material should be highly-absorbent sawdust or fine wood shavings. Untreated peat contains fungi and, if it gets damp, fungal growth may occur.

Location

The location of the cage is very important to the bird's well-being: the bird must have contact with the family, and it must be placed in a well-lit, draught-free place that also offers a shady retreat. To check for draughts, light a match or candle and observe the direction of the smoke: in draught-free areas, the smoke moves up vertically; in draughty places, it moves more horizontally. The number of places suitable for a cage is usually quite limited. The temperature in the kitchen fluctuates too much, and it holds too many dangers for safe flying exercise; the hall is too draughty; bedrooms are usually too quiet. Also, the bird should not be moved from room to room. So, the most logical place for a cage is often the living room - where the television set is located. Television light neither harms nor spoils your cockatiel, but the bird should be several metres away from the set and out of the direct line of the screen.

Lighting And Temperature

As mentioned above, the cage should be located in a well-lit spot that also offers shade. The normal light in a family home is sufficient. Many bird keepers disagree about whether or not the cage should be covered with a cloth, but covering it does protect the bird from chills. Make sure the cover lets in fresh air without allowing a draught, especially when it is hot. It should not be necessary to add artificial ultraviolet light.

Excessive heat is unnecessary and often even harmful. Birds have no sweat glands and their only method of heat regulation is to fluff their plumage and pant. Anything between 17 to 24°C (63 to 75°F) inside the room should be comfortable. Avoid extremes of temperature.

Exercise

Most cages are too small to allow cockatiels sufficient flying exercise, so your pet should be allowed regular flying time in a safe room. The Royal Society for the Prevention of Cruelty to Animals (RSPCA) considers it wrong to keep budgerigars permanently caged and what applies to budgerigars is surely also valid for cockatiels! A new bird needs to be acclimatised to its new environment and sufficiently tamed before you allow it to exercise in a room, otherwise it might become frightened and associate exercise with an unpleasant experience. Check the room for security and shut out other pets. Screen windows

All Cockateils enjoy regular out of cage exercise.

and doors, and neutralise dangerous areas such as water-filled vessels, open fires, hot stoves, narrow gaps behind furniture, fans, etc. Other dangerous spots are radiators, lamp shades, open drawers, spiny plants, and the gaps behind doors. Obviously, the kitchen, bathroom, a laundry room or workshop are totally unsuitable exercise rooms for birds. Make sure that there are no toxic materials (tobacco products, drugs, alcohol, chemicals, ointments, etc), or toxic plants (Christmas flower, lily of the valley, sanseviera, philodendron, cyclamen, oleander, azalea, daffodils, yew, juniper, privet, etc). The bird will not recognise all these substances as life threatening.

You have to expect damage to furniture, curtains, lamp shades, wallpapers and cables. The droppings of healthy cockatiels are dry and will be deposited only underneath selected perches, which you can protect accordingly. Cockatiels do not fly around restlessly but spend most of their time on a few vantage points.

Returning the bird to its cage may be a problem at the beginning. Do not feed the bird outside the cage, so that it learns that feed is available only inside its cage. It will usually return to its home without you having to catch it, if you have time and patience to wait. The cage door should always be open when the bird is out, with a perch in front of it. Do not catch the bird by hand. Finger-tame birds will allow owners to carry them to their cage.

Cages for cockatiels and parakeets are available in various basic designs, sizes, colours, and shapes. Your local pet shop will assist you in picking a cage that suits your bird.

A pied cockatiel

Cockatiels in an outdoor aviary.

Outdoor Aviary

Cockatiels can be kept in outdoor aviaries as long as certain conditions are met. Principally, outdoor aviaries should be draught-free and dry; they should face the sun and include a shaded, insulated shelter room. Avoid proximity to industrial smoke, busy and noisy traffic, pigeon lofts, other aviaries and poultry farms. Vermin and moist conditions are prevented by a sloping concrete floor and narrow gauge wire mesh but for cost reasons this type of construction is often rejected. Pea shingle which can be hosed down at regular intervals, or coarse sand which can be raked clean are both suitable alternatives to concrete and more ornamental. Rodents can be kept out by burying the mesh down to a depth of 30cm. The mesh around the bottom of the aviary should be fine or an overlaying double layer can be used.

The two layers should stop vermin, cat paws and wild birds from getting in, and prevent small birds from getting their heads stuck. Plastic coating on wire mesh is likely to be chewed off. Galvanized wire of the correct gauge (normally 19G) should be used. Cracks and crevices in wooden posts offer red mites an excellent hiding and breeding environment. Painting with non toxic paint or non toxic wood preserver at regular intervals should destroy such breeding grounds.

Outdoor aviaries should be partly covered by a roof, so that droppings from wild birds, which might contain pathogenic bacteria or parasites, are kept out as much as possible.

Covering only half the aviary roof allows the birds to bathe in light showers, but make sure access to shelter is always available in case of heavy rain. Feed and water containers should always be placed in the covered section. Under cold climatic conditions the drinking water could freeze and may cause a problem. Change the water frequently, use containers with heating elements or place drinkers in the shelter room.

Indoor Aviary

Indoor aviaries should be large enough to allow sufficient flying space to give adequate exercise. Like cages, indoor aviaries should be well lit, clean, draught-free, and heated if necessary. Artificial light and a dimmer for the night should be provided.

Cockatiels are endowed with a number of skills. They are excellent fliers and climbing acrobats; they can mimic simple words and whistle tunes. Their speech is simple and less distinct than that of some larger parrots or mynahs. If you want to teach your bird to talk, start with two-syllable words such as 'hello', 'coco', 'lady', etc. You will need a lot of patience, as you should not try to teach further words or phrases until the first words are repeated correctly. When teaching new words make sure that the first words are not forgotten.

Taming

Cockatiels are quite easy to tame while they are still young (a few months old) and single (without mate or partner). Taming pairs and older birds is much more difficult. Most authorities recommend wing clipping before starting the hand-taming process. Wing clipping should only be done by an experienced person. Taming is more difficult without wing clipping but it is still possible.

If your bird is tame, handling will not pose a problem.

Handling And Holding

Birds must sometimes be taken into the hand and held firmly, for example, during a close examination; when trimming the wings, upper beak and toenails; and when drugs have to be administered.

Handling a tamed bird does not pose a problem. However, handling a nervous adult biter can be quite stressful for both bird and owner. To handle an untame bird, put on a glove, close the windows, draw the curtains, dim the lights, and use a net or cloth to catch it. Talk to the bird in a quiet, calm voice, and do not approach it in a hurried or threatening manner.

The best way of handling a cockatiel is to close the palm of your hand over the bird's back and wings; and hold the head firmly between your thumb, index and middle finger.

As these are intelligent birds this is also a good time for human interaction and taming

Cage and cage furnishings require frequent cleaning to maintain hygienic conditions. This is particularly important for aviaries containing large numbers of birds. The disease risk can be reduced or minimised by proper hygiene, but it cannot be completely eliminated. Infectious agents have several ways of reaching their hosts - via feed (causing salmonellosis, pseudotuberculosis, fungi), water (coli enteritis, salmonellosis), air (viruses, pseudotuberculosis, fungi) and vermin (salmonellosis, pseudotuberculosis). It is obvious that hygiene cannot have any direct influence on metabolic diseases, but unhygienic conditions, and the stress that goes with them, are likely to make the birds more susceptible to such diseases.

Some of the necessary requirements for hygienic conditions are cleanliness, tidiness, clean air, waterproof or at least water-repellent materials, and smooth surfaces. It is much more difficult to keep clean a richly decorated bamboo cage than it is a modern cage with wire for the top and hard plastic for the bottom. Tidying up not only removes dust and dirt but also, and more importantly, allows for effective disinfection: disinfectants cannot work if the disease agents to be killed are covered, and thus protected, by dust, dirt, faeces and other organic matter.

CLEANING

Steps Towards Hygienic Conditions

1. Tidy up and remove grossly visible dirt, using a vacuum cleaner, shovel, scraper and wire brush.
2. Soak cage contents in water containing detergent or another mild cleaning agent for up to 24 hours.
3. Clean cage with hard brush, scraper, wire brush, water. Use steam-

A pied cockatiel on a natural perch. Perches cut from trees are better for your pet's feet.

NUTRITION

cleaning equipment if possible, especially in outdoor aviaries. (Steam cleans well but does not sterilise well as it cools too fast.)

4. Dry all materials, otherwise the water left from the previous steps would dilute the concentration of the disinfectants to be employed in the following step.

5. Disinfect cage and contents with one of the many disinfectants available from pet shops or chemists.

Most of the commercially-available disinfectants are effective against viruses, bacteria and fungi, but commonly less so against parasites. Active ingredients are usually aldehydes, alcohols, phenols, detergents, quaternary ammonium compounds, or a combination of these. Numerous brands are available and to name just a few of the most popular might prejudice against many others of similar effectiveness. If you are in doubt, ask your vet.

If your birds are infected with ectoparasites, such as red mites or feather mites, the animals and the aviary should be treated at the same time. The usual insecticides used for this purpose must be handled with great care as they are also toxic to people. The treatment for knemidokoptic mites, which cause 'scaly face' and 'scaly leg', is different because these parasites live permanently in, not on, the bird's skin.

The cockatiel eats mainly seeds, and its demands are relatively easy to satisfy. Pet shops offer a large variety of basic seeds and seed mixtures such as rearing feeds, titbits, vitamin mixtures and moulting aids.

NUTRITION

The cockatiel's basic diet consists predominantly of sunflower seeds, varying amounts of millet, canary seed, niger, husked and unhusked oats, wheat, peanuts, spray millet, small amounts of hemp, and so on.

This basic seed diet is supplemented by different types of fruit (apple, pear, berries, citrus, banana and other tropical fruits) and green food (dandelion blossoms and young dandelion leaves, chickweed, carrots and carrot leaves, lettuce, spinach, etc). Only the firm types of lettuce, such as endive and chicory, should be used. The cockatiel's diet is further supplemented by the bark of branches recommended earlier as natural perches. The bird chews the bark, which keeps it occupied and supplies it with vitamins and minerals.

You can replace some of the green food by sprouted seeds, particularly in winter time. Sprouted seeds are especially important for breeding birds as they are highly digestible and rich in vitamins. Soak the seeds in water in a strainer or in a humid container for about 24 hours. They must be kept in a warm place, such as in the kitchen or airing cupboard. After 24 hours rinse the seeds two or three times with tepid water and leave them standing for another day or two, until the sprouts are just visible. Thorough rinsing after the first 24 hours is important for hygienic reasons. The warm and moist conditions favour the growth of the fungi that are always present, even on top-quality seeds, and rinsing should wash most fungi away. Do not feed sprouted seeds which smell mouldy or which have visible fungal growth: they are likely to cause enteritis and fungal infections.

During the laying, breeding and rearing period, the bird's diet may be further supplemented by commercial rearing mixtures, wheat bread soaked in water, hard-boiled egg yolk, small amounts of dried shrimp, cottage cheese, and titbits such as honey sticks and seed rings. Some of these types of feed are perishable and must be removed from the cage after a couple of hours.

Vitamin preparations are not normally required if a well-balanced diet is given as described above. It is possible to overdose your bird with vitamins, particularly vitamins A and D. However, vitamins may be given for short periods when the bird is recovering from illness or a stressful situation. Let your veterinary surgeon work out the appropriate dosage.

The same rule applies to various types of stimulating

A cockatiel being hand feed using a spoon

drops and concoctions that are often advertised as an essential part of your bird's diet. They may boost your bird's resistance on a short-term basis but, given regularly and for extended periods, usually do not have a noticeably beneficial effect.

Further components of the diet are sand, grit, grated shells and cuttlebone. Grit helps the process of grinding up the husked seeds in the bird's gizzard. Grated shells and bits of cuttlebone are important sources of minerals for bone and eggshell formation.

Strongly salted or otherwise heavily seasoned human food, cheese, butter, chocolate, biscuits and 'junk' food should not be offered to cockatiels as they can cause diarrhoea and obesity.

Food Quality

The assessment of food quality is a difficult and sometimes uncertain task even for the expert. However, there are several tests that you can use to help you gauge the quality of the seed.

Reject any feed that is clumped, mouldy or wet and, of course, any that contains vermin or their droppings. Always check the date of manufacture or harvest

A white cockatiel with dark eyes. An albino cockatiel has pink eyes.

and also the country of origin. Put your nose close to the seed; spoiled feed has a stuffy, stale, rancid or pungent odour. Taste a few seeds; fresh seeds have a sweet taste. Make sure that the seed is not contaminated in any way. Sprout test a sample of the seed, employing the method of sprouting seed as described earlier; 80 to 90% of the fresh seeds should sprout. Oil test a sample of the seed; a fresh seed pressed on a sheet of paper will leave an oil spot, while a very old and dry seed will not. Rancid feed can be the result of prolonged storage, overheating during storage, direct sunlight, contamination with feed mites, and many other factors. It can deplete the bird of vitamins A and E and can cause enteritis.

Food Storage

All feed is perishable to a varying degree. Feed components can be metabolised by fermentation, bacteria, fungi and parasites. Some of these metabolised components are quite toxic, leading to diarrhoea, liver damage, deficiencies and other problems. Well-known examples of products that produce these undesirable effects are rancid fat and mouldy bread. Since feed spoilage is accelerated by light, high temperatures, high humidity and other factors, the rate of spoilage can be reduced by the following storage conditions:

1. Keep the feed cool, about 10 to 12°C (50 to 54°F) but not refrigerated, to reduce condensation.
2. Keep the feed dry, below 70% relative humidity, whenever possible. If conditions become very hot or humid, keep the feed in a ventilated place. Do not keep it in a tightly closed container for long periods.
3. Keep the feed in the dark, certainly away from direct sunlight which heats up the feed, causes fats to turn rancid, and inactivates the vitamins.
4. Keep the feed vermin-proof. Mice and rats are often carriers of disease agents (salmonellosis, pseudotuberculosis); feed mites cause fat to go rancid; weevils and moth larvae are less harmful but also undesirable contaminants.
5. Keep the feed for only a few months; buy fresh feed and check the date of its manufacture to ensure its freshness.

These precautions apply to the storage of seeds. Supplemental feed, such as fruit, egg yolk, cottage cheese and soaked bread should be removed and discarded after a few hours, depending on how warm or cold it is. Sprouted seeds must be prepared fresh every day.

Water

Water is essential for life. It should be clear, clean, tepid, and free of chlorine, disinfectants and any other additives. The chlorine gas in chlorinated water will escape if it is left standing in the open for a few hours. Disinfectants in very low concentrations are only justified if the water is not fit for human consumption. Disinfectants are irritants to the bird's intestines and may damage the natural gut

flora. Boiling the water before giving it to the birds is not recommended because boiled water tastes stale. If your water is of very poor quality, use still mineral water.

Change the drinking water at least twice a day, rinsing out the containers with clean fresh water on each occasion. Dirty drinking water supports the growth of certain bacteria, particularly coli bacteria, and can cause severe crop and intestinal infections, which are responsible for many deaths among cockatiels and other psittacine birds. Detergents should be used sparingly and must be rinsed off thoroughly because they can also irritate the bird's intestines and its bacterial flora.

It is often argued that drinking water is not very important for cockatiels because, in their natural habitat, they can survive without water for a few days. This statement is misleading and dangerous. If the drinking water is not changed frequently, particularly during hot spells, it will evaporate, leaving a thick and often stinking broth, which may cause severe enteritis in your birds. Would you, the bird keeper, consider drinking a stinking broth instead of clear water?

Feeding Technique

Food and water must be protected from faecal contamination. Most commercial feed containers are protected against such contamination by a hood. Feed containers should be clipped to the cage wire and should not be placed on the floor, although some breeders feel that feeding on the ground is the most natural and therefore the most desirable method. Perches must not be fitted directly above feed or water containers. In aviaries with several or many birds, the seeds that make up the basic diet will often be offered separately to reduce waste. Cockatiels, like many other psittacine birds, develop very individual preferences for certain seeds and will spill the other seeds out of the feed cup. Food containers must be checked daily.

Empty husks on the top may give the false impression that the container is still full so they must be gently blown away. Both the basic and supplemental feed, other than natural branches, should be changed daily.

Left: A 10-day-old hand-reared chick whose adult plumage is beginning to come through. Hand-reared birds become very tame.

PROBLEMS

There may well come a time when your bird is in need of professional help. Do not hesitate but go straight to the vet. Transport the bird in a small, softly padded, well-insulated and well-ventilated box or in a small cage covered with an insulating cloth. Post-veterinary treatment may include increased cage or aviary temperature, the use of infrared light, etc, depending on the disease or condition. If you have several birds, provide a 'hospital' or quarantine cage, to prevent the spread of disease and also to give the ailing bird some peace and quiet. Add an extra layer of sand at the bottom for the bird to sit on, and fit one perch close to the ground.

There are many diseases that can affect cockatiels, but fortunately few of them are fatal. However, since being aware of disease or problems is a vital concern of every bird fancier, here is a list of the more common and/or serious ones.

Colds: are characterised by a discharge from the nose, sneezing, fluffed plumage and loss of appetite. If left untreated, colds may go on to become serious respiratory diseases. Supply heat, avoid draughty locations for the cage and consult a vet.

Conjunctivitis: is an inflammation of the delicate membrane that lines the interior part of the eyelid and the exposed parts of the eye. It may be caused by colds, draughts, local infections and irritations, or respiratory diseases.

Crop disorders: often associated with diarrhoea, are common causes of vomiting and wasting in psittacine birds. Veterinary assistance should be sought.

Diarrhoea: can be a symptom of intestinal infections (enteritis), or can be caused by psittacosis, parasites and spoiled feed. Diarrhoea leads to quick dehydration and requires urgent treatment. The passing of excessive amounts of urates (polyuria) may be confused with diarrhoea. A dirty vent is a common sign of diarrhoea and kidney problems. Consult a veterinary surgeon as soon as possible.

Ectoparasites: are parasites living outside the host such as lice, mites, fleas and ticks. They are rare in cockatiels, but may be seen in crowded outdoor aviaries. Treat them with disinfectant solutions.

Egg-binding: is a condition in which the egg cannot pass through the oviduct. It leads to shock and local inflammation. If the egg is visible, apply oil and wait for the egg to be passed within a few minutes, otherwise see your vet immediately. Antibiotic treatment after the egg is removed may be very important.

Endoparasites: are parasites living inside the host, such as worms and flukes. They are rare in cockatiels kept indoors, but may occur in crowded outdoor aviaries; they require immediate treatment by a vet.

Right: A lutino displaying its fine crest.

Feather-plucking: is a common vice in larger parrots, but is rare in cockatiels. Possible causes are boredom and dietary deficiencies, to name just two. Give the bird plenty of green food, fruit, natural branches and attention.

Fluffed feathers: are a symptom of many infectious and non-infectious diseases. If keeping the bird warm, reducing draughts, etc, does not make any immediate difference, consult your vet as soon as possible.

Fractures: are the results of accidents and often the bird suffers from shock. It may be better to keep the bird in a quiet place for a short time, rather than splinting the fracture immediately. Fractures require the special knowledge of a vet.

Leg banding: is used by breeders to identify their birds. Closed rings can only be fitted to nestlings between the ages of four to ten days. Narrow rings may later grow into the leg and cause necrosis (death) of the tissue below the ring. To avoid this, regularly check that the ring still turns freely around the bird's leg.

Moulting: young cockatiels first moult at about six months, and thereafter once or twice a year. Moulting is a gradual process, taking place over several months and often is not noticed even by the owner. Consult your vet if your cockatiel gets 'stuck' in moult, as it may be caused by disease or nutritional deficiency. 'French moult' is a feathering abnormality caused by a virus and it requires veterinary care.

Obesity: is the excessive accumulation of fat and is related to overeating or to a lack of exercise, because the flying space is restricted. Encourage, but do not force, obese birds to fly and, of course, monitor and change their diet as necessary.

Old age: the life span of a captive cockatiel could be 12 to 14 years. An old bird may suffer from chronic heart failure and gout and often has difficulties perching. Lower the perches, move them closer together, and add extra sand to the floor.

Overgrown beaks: are a result of 'scaly face mites' (knemidokoptic mites) in budgerigars and of a viral disease in Yellow-crested cockatoos. Both diseases can occur in cockatiels, but they are rare. An overgrown beak interferes with proper husking of the seeds and preening. The beak must be trimmed by an experienced person because it may split or the bony structure may be injured.

Overgrown nails: are very common, particularly if exercise is limited and perches are not sized correctly. Hold the foot under a strong light and locate the blood line in each nail. Trim the nails with sharp clippers just below this point. It is best to have an experienced person help you the first few times you do this.

Poisoning: is often caused by the bird eating plants, human foods, or investigating things around the home. If you suspect that your bird has ingested anything poisonous, take it to the vet immediately.

Psittacosis: is caused by a virus-like infectious agent. Affected birds may not show recognisable symptoms or they may show general malaise with dyspnoea (difficulty in breathing), discharge from eyes or nose, or diarrhoea. Humans can catch psittacosis from birds and, needless to say, prompt professional treatment is necessary.

Respiratory diseases: in cockatiels are usually the result of infections, such as colds, aspergillosis, psittacosis. Consult a veterinary surgeon.

Salmonellosis or paratyphoid enteritis: is a bacterial disease that causes general septicemia, hepatitis and enteritis. The disease is transmissible from, and to, man. It is transmitted orally from infected feed or droppings from birds or vermin. The disease can prove quite a problem in highly stocked aviaries, but is uncommon in single birds.

Vomiting: may be a sign of crop infection and requires urgent veterinary attention. The bird may also show loose droppings (diarrhoea) and may lose weight.

Wounds: are usually the result of accidents or fights. Small wounds should be left alone, larger ones may need stitching or other forms of treatment. Separate fighting birds by removing the aggressor.

Wing clipping: if done correctly, wing clipping is a painless method to render birds flightless until their feathers regrow (after approximately six months). The most widely-used method is to leave the outer

Cockatiels are normally quite peaceful birds, but there may be arguments about partners and good nesting spots.

two primary flight feathers and to cut the others. It is important not to clip closer to the wing than the length of the coverts, otherwise the quills may split and ingrowing feathers may result. It is advisable to watch an experienced person do this for the first few times.

33

BIBLIOGRAPHY

THE PROPER CARE OF COCKATIELS
by Karl-Herbert Delpy
TW-105S
ISBN 0-79383-150-4
Clearly written and illustrated throughout with full-colour photographs, The Proper Care of Cockatiels provides readers with all the basics of cockatiel ownership, including feeding, housing and health care. It also discusses how to breed cockatiels and raise the young.
Hardcover: 185 x 130 mm, 256 pages, full-colour illustrations throughout.

COCKATIELS - AS A HOBBY
by Jack C Harris
TT-007
ISBN 0-86622-423-8
An easy-to-read and colourful introduction to the cockatiel, covering everything that the fancier needs to know, including an extended section on breeding. This book is a Save-Our-Planet book, and all profits go towards preserving the virgin rain forests of Brazil.
Softcover: 250 x 170 mm, 98 pages, full-colour throughout.

COCKATIELS!
PETS - BREEDING - SHOWING
by Nancy A Reed
TS-140
ISBN 0-86622-640-0
Nancy Reed has written a comprehensive work on the cockatiel, which contains the good advice and tips that have made her own birds consistent winners. With contributions from avian experts on illnesses and colour mutations, this book is a must for the serious breeder.
Hardcover: 218 x 140 mm, 256 pages, 97 full-colour photographs throughout.

COCKATIELS AS A NEW PET
by John Coborn
TU-005
ISBN 0-86622-612-5
Designed specifically for use by beginners, this book covers those subjects which are of particular concern and interest to the new fancier. Lavish use of photographs show the brilliant range of colours available to the cockatiel owner.
Softcover: 214 x 170 mm, 64 pages, full-colour photographs throughout.

USEFUL ADDRESSES

Royal Society for the Prevention of Cruelty to Animals
(RSPCA)
Causeway, Horsham
West Sussex   RH12 IHG
Tel: 01403 264181
Website: www.rspca.org.uk

National Council for Aviculture
4 Haven Crescent
Werrington, Stoke-on-Trent
Staffordshire   ST9 0EY
Website: www.netcomuk.co.uk/~ncabirds/NCA.htm